THIS JOURNAL

Belongs To:

My BOOK CLUB Journal

A READING LOG OF THE BOOKS I LOVED,
LOATHED, AND COULDN'T WAIT TO TALK ABOUT

weldonowen

HOW TO USE THIS BOOK

Welcome to your book club journal, a place to record everything about books you've read in groups (or alone!).

This book is divided into three parts. In the first section, Reading Logs provide space to record in-depth notes on the selected titles. An overview section with lines to record general details such as title, author, first thoughts, final impressions, and ratings, allows readers to brush up on past reads. Following the overview are blank pages for recording general notes and questions to help prompt conversation during discussions.

The second section contains the personalized Reading Log Index. Here, you have a place to record the at-a-glance details about your reads. Each log entry includes spaces for key information, such as the title, author, read date, rating, and the page number that corresponds to the book's detailed entry.

The final section is an at-a-glance guide to starting your own book club, with tips and tricks to help you keep your members engaged, and a list of recommended reads to guide you toward new genres and authors.

Happy reading!

READING LOGS

Title

Author

Genre

Format: ○ Paper ○ E-book ○ Audio

Where/When Read ____________________

FIRST THOUGHTS

FINAL IMPRESSIONS

RATINGS

Characters	Plot	Writing	Overall
☆☆☆☆☆	☆☆☆☆☆	☆☆☆☆☆	☆☆☆☆☆

Recommend: ○ Yes ○ No Why:

NOTES & QUESTIONS

NOTES & QUESTIONS

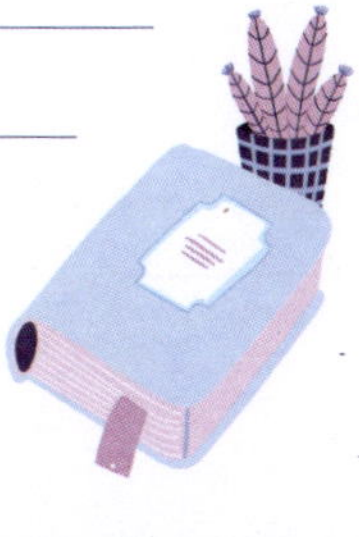

READING LOGS

Title

Author

Genre

Format: ○ Paper ○ E-book ○ Audio

Where/When Read ______

FIRST THOUGHTS ______

FINAL IMPRESSIONS ______

RATINGS

Characters	Plot	Writing	Overall
☆☆☆☆☆	☆☆☆☆☆	☆☆☆☆☆	☆☆☆☆☆

Recommend: ○ Yes ○ No Why: ______

NOTES & QUESTIONS

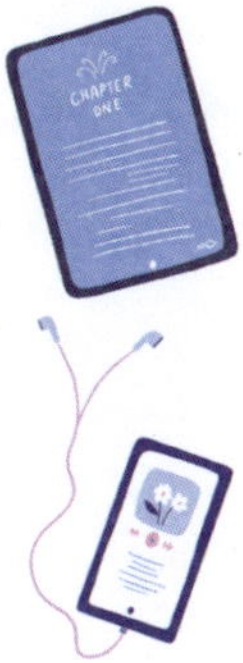

NOTES & QUESTIONS

READING LOGS

Title

Author

Genre

Format: ○ Paper ○ E-book ○ Audio

Where/When Read ____________________

FIRST THOUGHTS

FINAL IMPRESSIONS

RATINGS

Characters	Plot	Writing	Overall
☆☆☆☆☆	☆☆☆☆☆	☆☆☆☆☆	☆☆☆☆☆

Recommend: ○ Yes ○ No Why: ____________________

NOTES & QUESTIONS

NOTES & QUESTIONS

READING LOGS

Title

Author

Genre

Format: ◯ Paper ◯ E-book ◯ Audio

Where/When Read ______________________

FIRST THOUGHTS ______________________

FINAL IMPRESSIONS ______________________

RATINGS

Characters	Plot	Writing	Overall
☆☆☆☆☆	☆☆☆☆☆	☆☆☆☆☆	☆☆☆☆☆

Recommend: ◯ Yes ◯ No Why: ______________________

NOTES & QUESTIONS

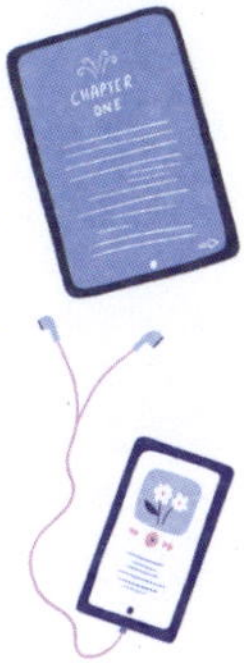

NOTES & QUESTIONS

READING LOGS

Title

Author

Genre

Format: ○ Paper ○ E-book ○ Audio

Where/When Read ______________________

FIRST THOUGHTS

____

FINAL IMPRESSIONS

____

RATINGS

Characters	Plot	Writing	Overall
☆☆☆☆☆	☆☆☆☆☆	☆☆☆☆☆	☆☆☆☆☆

Recommend: ○ Yes ○ No Why: ______________________

NOTES & QUESTIONS

NOTES & QUESTIONS

READING LOGS

Title

Author

Genre

Format: ○ Paper ○ E-book ○ Audio

Where/When Read ______________________

FIRST THOUGHTS ______________________

FINAL IMPRESSIONS ______________________

RATINGS

Characters	Plot	Writing	Overall
☆☆☆☆☆	☆☆☆☆☆	☆☆☆☆☆	☆☆☆☆☆

Recommend: ○ Yes ○ No Why: ______________________

NOTES & QUESTIONS

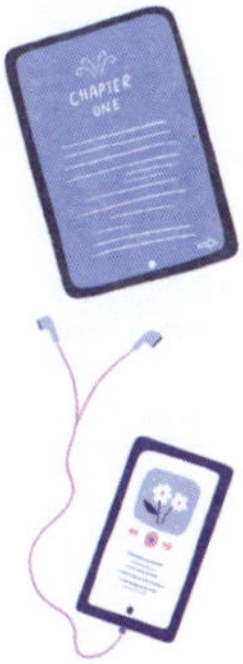

NOTES & QUESTIONS

READING LOGS

Title

Author

Genre

Format: ○ Paper ○ E-book ○ Audio

Where/When Read ______________________

FIRST THOUGHTS

____

FINAL IMPRESSIONS

____

RATINGS

Characters	Plot	Writing	Overall
☆☆☆☆☆	☆☆☆☆☆	☆☆☆☆☆	☆☆☆☆☆

Recommend: ○ Yes ○ No Why: ______________________

NOTES & QUESTIONS

NOTES & QUESTIONS

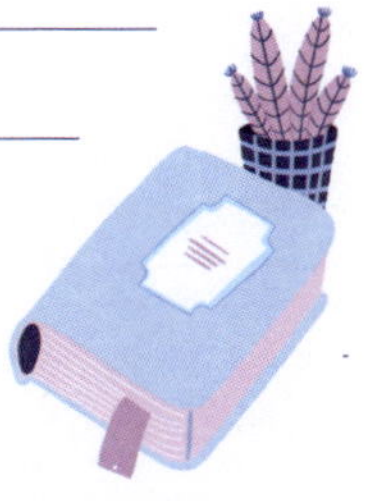

READING LOGS

Title

Author

Genre

Format: ○ Paper ○ E-book ○ Audio

Where/When Read ______

FIRST THOUGHTS ______

FINAL IMPRESSIONS ______

RATINGS

Characters	Plot	Writing	Overall
☆☆☆☆☆	☆☆☆☆☆	☆☆☆☆☆	☆☆☆☆☆

Recommend: ○ Yes ○ No Why: ______

NOTES & QUESTIONS

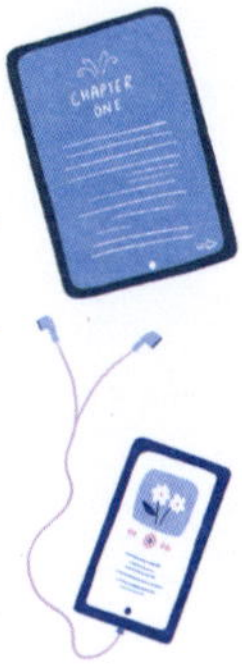

NOTES & QUESTIONS

READING LOGS

Title

Author

Genre

Format: ○ Paper ○ E-book ○ Audio

Where/When Read ______________________

FIRST THOUGHTS ______________________

FINAL IMPRESSIONS ______________________

RATINGS

Characters	Plot	Writing	Overall
☆☆☆☆☆	☆☆☆☆☆	☆☆☆☆☆	☆☆☆☆☆

Recommend: ○ Yes ○ No Why: ______________________

NOTES & QUESTIONS

NOTES & QUESTIONS

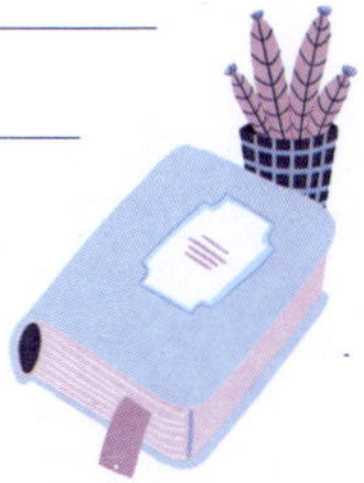

READING LOGS

Title

Author

Genre

Format: ○ Paper ○ E-book ○ Audio

Where/When Read ______

FIRST THOUGHTS ______

FINAL IMPRESSIONS ______

RATINGS

Characters	Plot	Writing	Overall
☆☆☆☆☆	☆☆☆☆☆	☆☆☆☆☆	☆☆☆☆☆

Recommend: ○ Yes ○ No Why: ______

NOTES & QUESTIONS

NOTES & QUESTIONS

READING LOGS

Title

Author

Genre

Format: ○ Paper ○ E-book ○ Audio

Where/When Read ______

FIRST THOUGHTS ______

FINAL IMPRESSIONS ______

RATINGS

Characters	Plot	Writing	Overall
☆☆☆☆☆	☆☆☆☆☆	☆☆☆☆☆	☆☆☆☆☆

Recommend: ○ Yes ○ No Why: ______

NOTES & QUESTIONS

NOTES & QUESTIONS

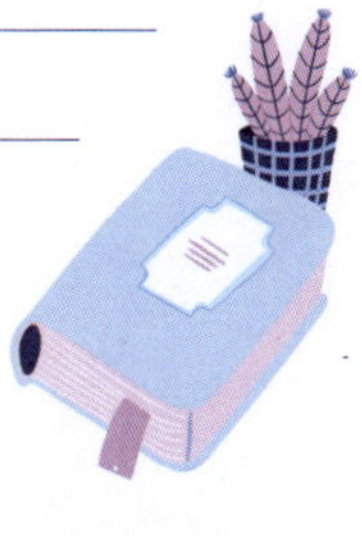

READING LOGS

Title

Author

Genre

Format: ○ Paper ○ E-book ○ Audio

Where/When Read ______________________

FIRST THOUGHTS ______________________

FINAL IMPRESSIONS ______________________

RATINGS

Characters	Plot	Writing	Overall
☆☆☆☆☆	☆☆☆☆☆	☆☆☆☆☆	☆☆☆☆☆

Recommend: ○ Yes ○ No Why: ______________________

NOTES & QUESTIONS

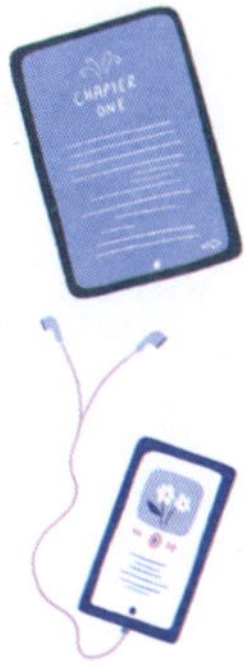

NOTES & QUESTIONS

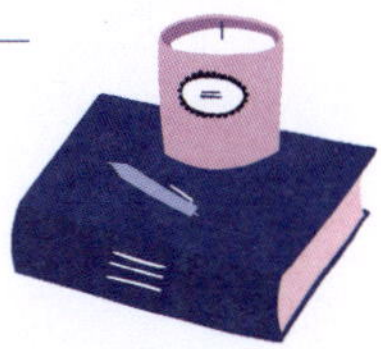

READING LOGS

Title

Author

Genre

Format: ○ Paper ○ E-book ○ Audio

Where/When Read ______________________

FIRST THOUGHTS ______________________

FINAL IMPRESSIONS ______________________

RATINGS

Characters	Plot	Writing	Overall
☆☆☆☆☆	☆☆☆☆☆	☆☆☆☆☆	☆☆☆☆☆

Recommend: ○ Yes ○ No Why: ______________________

NOTES & QUESTIONS

NOTES & QUESTIONS

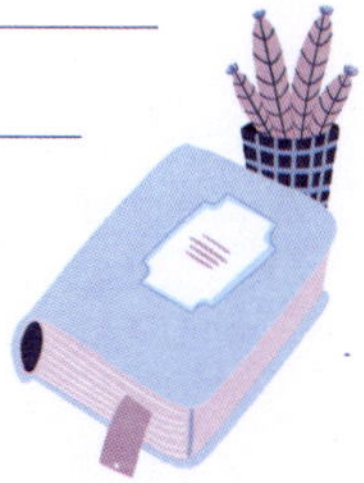

READING LOGS

Title

Author

Genre

Format: ○ Paper ○ E-book ○ Audio

Where/When Read ______________________

FIRST THOUGHTS ______________________

FINAL IMPRESSIONS ______________________

RATINGS

Characters	Plot	Writing	Overall
☆☆☆☆☆	☆☆☆☆☆	☆☆☆☆☆	☆☆☆☆☆

Recommend: ○ Yes ○ No Why: ______________________

NOTES & QUESTIONS

NOTES & QUESTIONS

READING LOGS

Title

Author

Genre

Format: ○ Paper ○ E-book ○ Audio

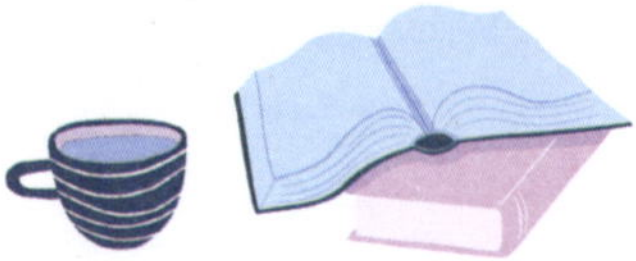

Where/When Read ____________________

FIRST THOUGHTS ____________________

FINAL IMPRESSIONS ____________________

RATINGS

Characters	Plot	Writing	Overall
☆☆☆☆☆	☆☆☆☆☆	☆☆☆☆☆	☆☆☆☆☆

Recommend: ○ Yes ○ No Why: ____________________

NOTES & QUESTIONS

NOTES & QUESTIONS

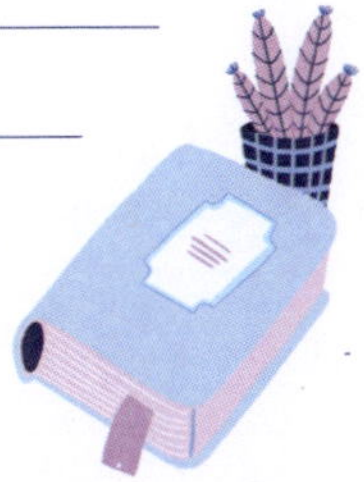

READING LOGS

Title

Author

Genre

Format: ○ Paper ○ E-book ○ Audio

Where/When Read ______________________

FIRST THOUGHTS

FINAL IMPRESSIONS

RATINGS

Characters	Plot	Writing	Overall
☆☆☆☆☆	☆☆☆☆☆	☆☆☆☆☆	☆☆☆☆☆

Recommend: ○ Yes ○ No Why: ______________________

NOTES & QUESTIONS

NOTES & QUESTIONS

READING LOGS

Title

Author

Genre

Format: ◯ Paper ◯ E-book ◯ Audio

Where/When Read ______

FIRST THOUGHTS

FINAL IMPRESSIONS

RATINGS

Characters	Plot	Writing	Overall
☆☆☆☆☆	☆☆☆☆☆	☆☆☆☆☆	☆☆☆☆☆

Recommend: ◯ Yes ◯ No Why: ______

NOTES & QUESTIONS

NOTES & QUESTIONS

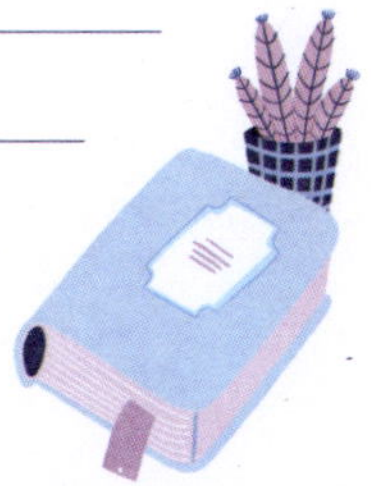

READING LOGS

Title

Author

Genre

Format: ○ Paper ○ E-book ○ Audio

Where/When Read ____________________

FIRST THOUGHTS

FINAL IMPRESSIONS

RATINGS

Characters	Plot	Writing	Overall
☆☆☆☆☆	☆☆☆☆☆	☆☆☆☆☆	☆☆☆☆☆

Recommend: ○ Yes ○ No Why: ____________________

NOTES & QUESTIONS

NOTES & QUESTIONS

READING LOGS

Title

Author

Genre

Format: ○ Paper ○ E-book ○ Audio

Where/When Read ______________________

FIRST THOUGHTS

____

FINAL IMPRESSIONS

____

RATINGS

Characters	Plot	Writing	Overall
☆☆☆☆☆	☆☆☆☆☆	☆☆☆☆☆	☆☆☆☆☆

Recommend: ○ Yes ○ No Why: ______________________

NOTES & QUESTIONS

NOTES & QUESTIONS

READING LOGS

Title

Author

Genre

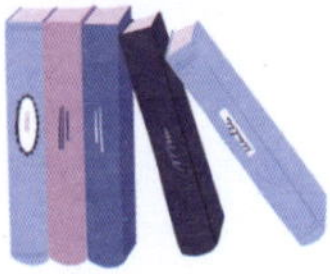

Format: ○ Paper ○ E-book ○ Audio

Where/When Read ______

FIRST THOUGHTS ______

FINAL IMPRESSIONS ______

RATINGS

Characters	Plot	Writing	Overall
☆☆☆☆☆	☆☆☆☆☆	☆☆☆☆☆	☆☆☆☆☆

Recommend: ○ Yes ○ No Why: ______

NOTES & QUESTIONS

NOTES & QUESTIONS

READING LOGS

Title

Author

Genre

Format: ○ Paper ○ E-book ○ Audio

Where/When Read ______

FIRST THOUGHTS

FINAL IMPRESSIONS

RATINGS

Characters	Plot	Writing	Overall
☆☆☆☆☆	☆☆☆☆☆	☆☆☆☆☆	☆☆☆☆☆

Recommend: ○ Yes ○ No Why: ______

NOTES & QUESTIONS

NOTES & QUESTIONS

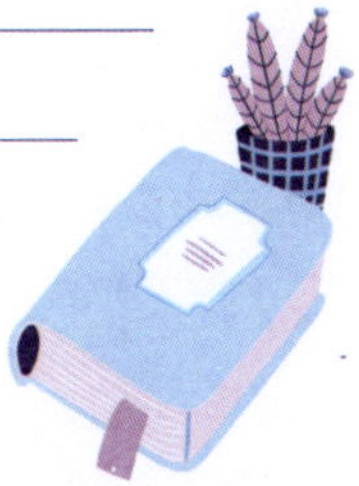

READING LOGS

Title

Author

Genre

Format: ○ Paper ○ E-book ○ Audio

Where/When Read ____________________

FIRST THOUGHTS ____________________

____

____

____

____

FINAL IMPRESSIONS ____________________

____

____

____

RATINGS

Characters	Plot	Writing	Overall
☆☆☆☆☆	☆☆☆☆☆	☆☆☆☆☆	☆☆☆☆☆

Recommend: ○ Yes ○ No Why: ____________________

____

____

NOTES & QUESTIONS

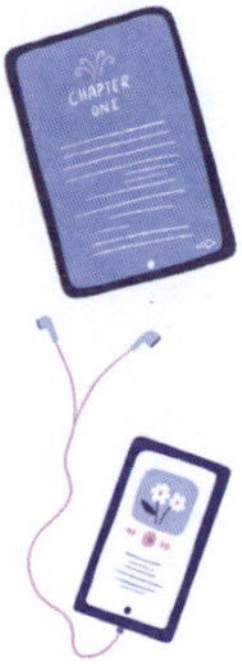

NOTES & QUESTIONS

READING LOGS

Title

Author

Genre

Format: ○ Paper ○ E-book ○ Audio

Where/When Read ______________________

FIRST THOUGHTS ______________________

____

____

____

____

FINAL IMPRESSIONS ______________________

____

____

____

RATINGS

Characters	Plot	Writing	Overall
☆☆☆☆☆	☆☆☆☆☆	☆☆☆☆☆	☆☆☆☆☆

Recommend: ○ Yes ○ No Why: ______________________

____

____

NOTES & QUESTIONS

NOTES & QUESTIONS

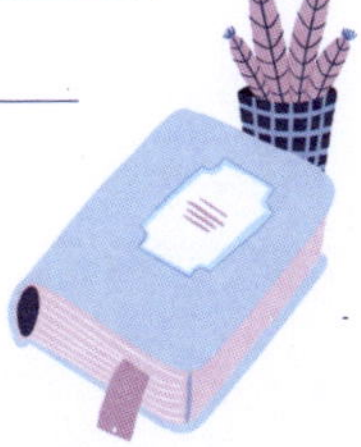

READING LOGS

Title

Author

Genre

Format: ○ Paper ○ E-book ○ Audio

Where/When Read ______________________

FIRST THOUGHTS

____

____

____

____

FINAL IMPRESSIONS

____

____

____

RATINGS

Characters	Plot	Writing	Overall
☆☆☆☆☆	☆☆☆☆☆	☆☆☆☆☆	☆☆☆☆☆

Recommend: ○ Yes ○ No Why: ______________________

____

____

NOTES & QUESTIONS

NOTES & QUESTIONS

READING LOGS

Title

Author

Genre

Format: ○ Paper ○ E-book ○ Audio

Where/When Read ______

FIRST THOUGHTS

______

FINAL IMPRESSIONS

______

RATINGS

Characters	Plot	Writing	Overall
☆☆☆☆☆	☆☆☆☆☆	☆☆☆☆☆	☆☆☆☆☆

Recommend: ○ Yes ○ No Why: ______

NOTES & QUESTIONS

NOTES & QUESTIONS

READING LOGS

Title

Author

Genre

Format: ○ Paper ○ E-book ○ Audio

Where/When Read ____________________

FIRST THOUGHTS ____________________

____

____

____

____

FINAL IMPRESSIONS ____________________

____

____

____

RATINGS

Characters	Plot	Writing	Overall
☆☆☆☆☆	☆☆☆☆☆	☆☆☆☆☆	☆☆☆☆☆

Recommend: ○ Yes ○ No Why: ____________________

____

____

NOTES & QUESTIONS

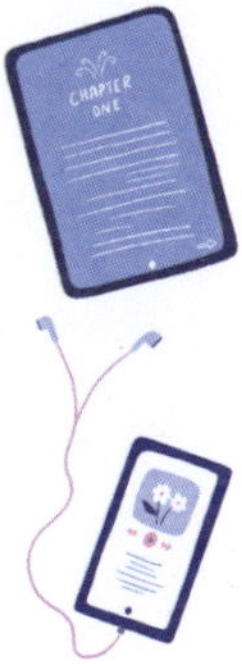

NOTES & QUESTIONS

READING LOGS

Title

Author

Genre

Format: ○ Paper ○ E-book ○ Audio

Where/When Read ____________________

FIRST THOUGHTS ____________________

FINAL IMPRESSIONS ____________________

RATINGS

Characters	Plot	Writing	Overall
☆☆☆☆☆	☆☆☆☆☆	☆☆☆☆☆	☆☆☆☆☆

Recommend: ○ Yes ○ No Why: ____________________

NOTES & QUESTIONS

NOTES & QUESTIONS

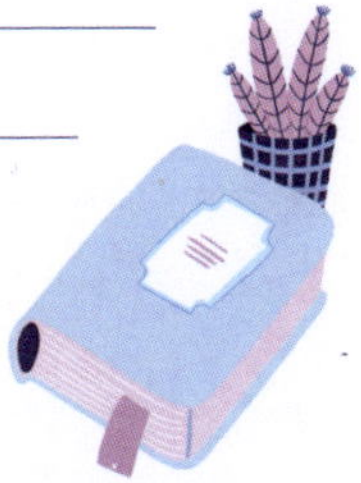

READING LOGS

Title

Author

Genre

Format: ○ Paper ○ E-book ○ Audio

Where/When Read ______________________

FIRST THOUGHTS ______________________

FINAL IMPRESSIONS ______________________

RATINGS

Characters	Plot	Writing	Overall
☆☆☆☆☆	☆☆☆☆☆	☆☆☆☆☆	☆☆☆☆☆

Recommend: ○ Yes ○ No Why: ______________________

NOTES & QUESTIONS

NOTES & QUESTIONS

READING LOGS

Title

Author

Genre

Format: ○ Paper ○ E-book ○ Audio

Where/When Read ______________________

FIRST THOUGHTS ______________________

____

____

____

____

FINAL IMPRESSIONS ______________________

____

____

____

RATINGS

Characters	Plot	Writing	Overall
☆☆☆☆☆	☆☆☆☆☆	☆☆☆☆☆	☆☆☆☆☆

Recommend: ○ Yes ○ No Why: ______________________

____

____

NOTES & QUESTIONS

NOTES & QUESTIONS

READING LOGS

Title

Author

Genre

Format: ○ Paper ○ E-book ○ Audio

Where/When Read ____________________

FIRST THOUGHTS ____________________

____

____

____

____

FINAL IMPRESSIONS ____________________

____

____

____

RATINGS

Characters	Plot	Writing	Overall
☆☆☆☆☆	☆☆☆☆☆	☆☆☆☆☆	☆☆☆☆☆

Recommend: ○ Yes ○ No Why: ____________________

____

____

NOTES & QUESTIONS

NOTES & QUESTIONS

READING LOGS

Title

Author

Genre

Format: ○ Paper ○ E-book ○ Audio

Where/When Read ______________________

FIRST THOUGHTS ______________________

____

____

____

____

FINAL IMPRESSIONS ______________________

____

____

____

RATINGS

Characters	Plot	Writing	Overall
☆☆☆☆☆	☆☆☆☆☆	☆☆☆☆☆	☆☆☆☆☆

Recommend: ○ Yes ○ No Why: ______________________

____

____

NOTES & QUESTIONS

NOTES & QUESTIONS

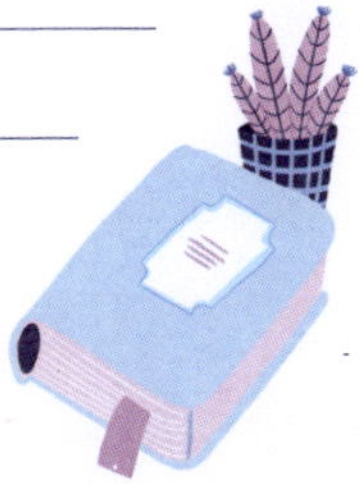

READING LOGS

Title

Author

Genre

Format: ○ Paper ○ E-book ○ Audio

Where/When Read ______________________

FIRST THOUGHTS ______________________

FINAL IMPRESSIONS ______________________

RATINGS

Characters	Plot	Writing	Overall
☆☆☆☆☆	☆☆☆☆☆	☆☆☆☆☆	☆☆☆☆☆

Recommend: ○ Yes ○ No Why: ______________________

NOTES & QUESTIONS

NOTES & QUESTIONS

READING LOGS

Title

Author

Genre

Format: ○ Paper ○ E-book ○ Audio

Where/When Read ______

FIRST THOUGHTS ______

FINAL IMPRESSIONS ______

RATINGS

Characters	Plot	Writing	Overall
☆☆☆☆☆	☆☆☆☆☆	☆☆☆☆☆	☆☆☆☆☆

Recommend: ○ Yes ○ No Why: ______

NOTES & QUESTIONS

NOTES & QUESTIONS

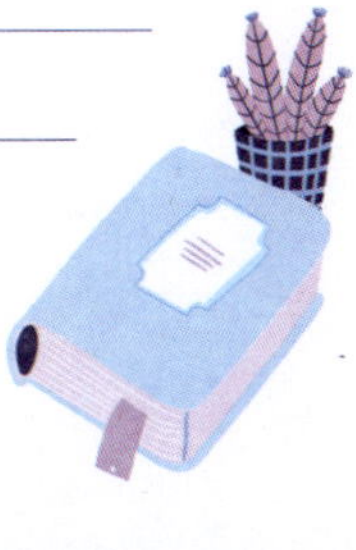

READING LOGS

Title

Author

Genre

Format: ○ Paper ○ E-book ○ Audio

Where/When Read ______

FIRST THOUGHTS ______

FINAL IMPRESSIONS ______

RATINGS

Characters	Plot	Writing	Overall
☆☆☆☆☆	☆☆☆☆☆	☆☆☆☆☆	☆☆☆☆☆

Recommend: ○ Yes ○ No Why: ______

NOTES & QUESTIONS

NOTES & QUESTIONS

READING LOGS

Title

Author

Genre

Format: ◯ Paper ◯ E-book ◯ Audio

Where/When Read ______

FIRST THOUGHTS ______

FINAL IMPRESSIONS ______

RATINGS

Characters	Plot	Writing	Overall
☆☆☆☆☆	☆☆☆☆☆	☆☆☆☆☆	☆☆☆☆☆

Recommend: ◯ Yes ◯ No Why: ______

NOTES & QUESTIONS

NOTES & QUESTIONS

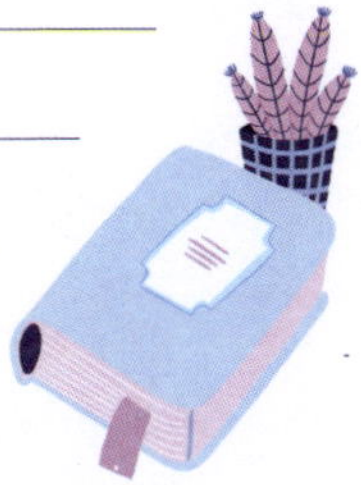

READING LOGS

Title

Author

Genre

Format: ○ Paper ○ E-book ○ Audio

Where/When Read ______________________

FIRST THOUGHTS ______________________

FINAL IMPRESSIONS ______________________

RATINGS

Characters	Plot	Writing	Overall
☆☆☆☆☆	☆☆☆☆☆	☆☆☆☆☆	☆☆☆☆☆

Recommend: ○ Yes ○ No Why: ______________________

NOTES & QUESTIONS

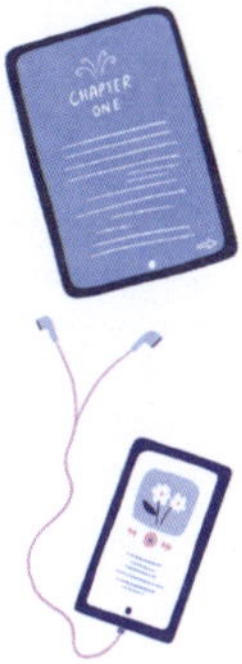

NOTES & QUESTIONS

READING LOGS

Title

Author

Genre

Format: ○ Paper ○ E-book ○ Audio

Where/When Read ____________________

FIRST THOUGHTS

FINAL IMPRESSIONS

RATINGS

Characters	Plot	Writing	Overall
☆☆☆☆☆	☆☆☆☆☆	☆☆☆☆☆	☆☆☆☆☆

Recommend: ○ Yes ○ No Why: ____________________

NOTES & QUESTIONS

NOTES & QUESTIONS

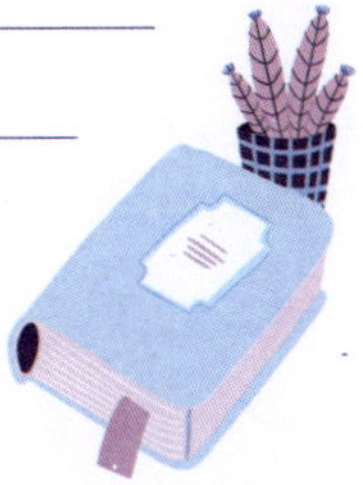

READING LOGS

Title

Author

Genre

Format: ○ Paper ○ E-book ○ Audio

Where/When Read ______________________

FIRST THOUGHTS

____

FINAL IMPRESSIONS

____

RATINGS

Characters	Plot	Writing	Overall
☆☆☆☆☆	☆☆☆☆☆	☆☆☆☆☆	☆☆☆☆☆

Recommend: ○ Yes ○ No Why: ______________________

NOTES & QUESTIONS

NOTES & QUESTIONS

READING LOGS

Title

Author

Genre

Format: ○ Paper ○ E-book ○ Audio

Where/When Read ______

FIRST THOUGHTS

______

FINAL IMPRESSIONS

______

RATINGS

Characters	**Plot**	**Writing**	**Overall**
☆☆☆☆☆	☆☆☆☆☆	☆☆☆☆☆	☆☆☆☆☆

Recommend: ○ Yes ○ No Why: ______

NOTES & QUESTIONS

NOTES & QUESTIONS

READING LOGS

Title

Author

Genre

Format: ○ Paper ○ E-book ○ Audio

Where/When Read ______

FIRST THOUGHTS

______

FINAL IMPRESSIONS

______

RATINGS

Characters	Plot	Writing	Overall
☆☆☆☆☆	☆☆☆☆☆	☆☆☆☆☆	☆☆☆☆☆

Recommend: ○ Yes ○ No Why: ______

NOTES & QUESTIONS

NOTES & QUESTIONS

READING LOGS

Title

Author

Genre

Format: ○ Paper ○ E-book ○ Audio

Where/When Read ____________________

FIRST THOUGHTS ____________________

FINAL IMPRESSIONS ____________________

RATINGS

Characters	Plot	Writing	Overall
☆☆☆☆☆	☆☆☆☆☆	☆☆☆☆☆	☆☆☆☆☆

Recommend: ○ Yes ○ No Why: ____________________

NOTES & QUESTIONS

NOTES & QUESTIONS

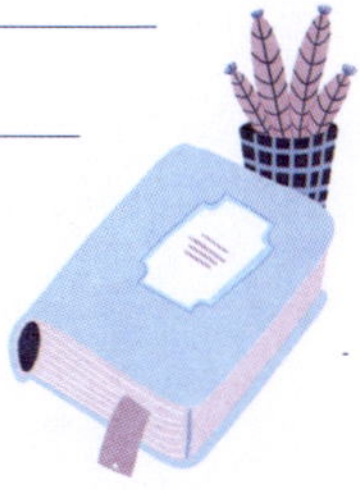

READING LOGS

Title

Author

Genre

Format: ○ Paper ○ E-book ○ Audio

Where/When Read ______________________

FIRST THOUGHTS ______________________

____

____

____

____

FINAL IMPRESSIONS ______________________

____

____

____

RATINGS

Characters	Plot	Writing	Overall
☆☆☆☆☆	☆☆☆☆☆	☆☆☆☆☆	☆☆☆☆☆

Recommend: ○ Yes ○ No Why: ______________________

____

____

NOTES & QUESTIONS

NOTES & QUESTIONS

READING LOGS

Title

Author

Genre

Format: ○ Paper ○ E-book ○ Audio

Where/When Read ______________________

FIRST THOUGHTS ______________________

____

____

____

____

FINAL IMPRESSIONS ______________________

____

____

____

RATINGS

Characters	Plot	Writing	Overall
☆☆☆☆☆	☆☆☆☆☆	☆☆☆☆☆	☆☆☆☆☆

Recommend: ○ Yes ○ No Why: ______________________

____

____

NOTES & QUESTIONS

NOTES & QUESTIONS

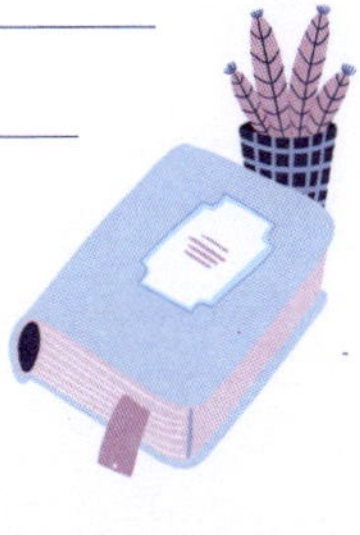

READING LOGS

Title

Author

Genre

Format: ○ Paper ○ E-book ○ Audio

Where/When Read ____________________

FIRST THOUGHTS ____________________

FINAL IMPRESSIONS ____________________

RATINGS

Characters	Plot	Writing	Overall
☆☆☆☆☆	☆☆☆☆☆	☆☆☆☆☆	☆☆☆☆☆

Recommend: ○ Yes ○ No Why: ____________________

NOTES & QUESTIONS

NOTES & QUESTIONS

READING LOGS

Title

Author

Genre

Format: ○ Paper ○ E-book ○ Audio

Where/When Read ______

FIRST THOUGHTS

FINAL IMPRESSIONS

RATINGS

Characters	Plot	Writing	Overall
☆☆☆☆☆	☆☆☆☆☆	☆☆☆☆☆	☆☆☆☆☆

Recommend: ○ Yes ○ No Why: ______

NOTES & QUESTIONS

NOTES & QUESTIONS

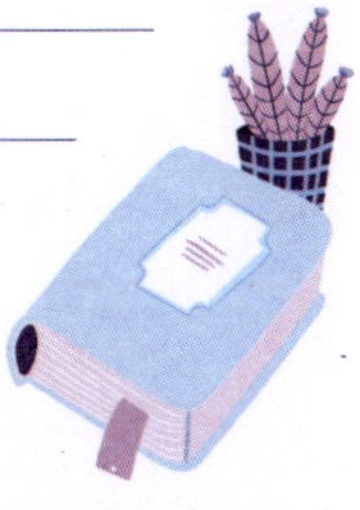

READING LOGS

Title

Author

Genre

Format: ○ Paper ○ E-book ○ Audio

Where/When Read ______________________

FIRST THOUGHTS

____

____

____

____

FINAL IMPRESSIONS

____

____

____

RATINGS

Characters	Plot	Writing	Overall
☆☆☆☆☆	☆☆☆☆☆	☆☆☆☆☆	☆☆☆☆☆

Recommend: ○ Yes ○ No Why: ______________________

____

____

NOTES & QUESTIONS

NOTES & QUESTIONS

READING LOGS

Title

Author

Genre

Format: ○ Paper ○ E-book ○ Audio

Where/When Read ______________________

FIRST THOUGHTS ______________________

____

____

____

____

FINAL IMPRESSIONS ______________________

____

____

____

RATINGS

Characters	**Plot**	**Writing**	**Overall**
☆☆☆☆☆	☆☆☆☆☆	☆☆☆☆☆	☆☆☆☆☆

Recommend: ○ Yes ○ No Why: ______________________

____

____

NOTES & QUESTIONS

NOTES & QUESTIONS

READING LOGS

Title

Author

Genre

Format: ○ Paper ○ E-book ○ Audio

Where/When Read ____________________

FIRST THOUGHTS ____________________

____

____

____

____

FINAL IMPRESSIONS ____________________

____

____

____

RATINGS

Characters	Plot	Writing	Overall
☆☆☆☆☆	☆☆☆☆☆	☆☆☆☆☆	☆☆☆☆☆

Recommend: ○ Yes ○ No Why: ____________________

____

____

NOTES & QUESTIONS

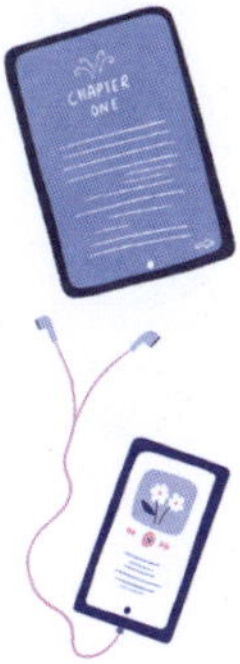

NOTES & QUESTIONS

READING LOGS

Title

Author

Genre

Format: ○ Paper ○ E-book ○ Audio

Where/When Read ______________________

FIRST THOUGHTS ______________________

FINAL IMPRESSIONS ______________________

RATINGS

Characters	Plot	Writing	Overall
☆☆☆☆☆	☆☆☆☆☆	☆☆☆☆☆	☆☆☆☆☆

Recommend: ○ Yes ○ No Why: ______________________

NOTES & QUESTIONS

NOTES & QUESTIONS

READING LOGS

Title

Author

Genre

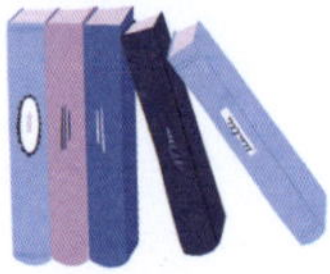

Format: ○ Paper ○ E-book ○ Audio

Where/When Read ______________________

FIRST THOUGHTS

____

____

____

____

FINAL IMPRESSIONS

____

____

____

RATINGS

Characters	Plot	Writing	Overall
☆☆☆☆☆	☆☆☆☆☆	☆☆☆☆☆	☆☆☆☆☆

Recommend: ○ Yes ○ No Why: ______________________

____

____

NOTES & QUESTIONS

NOTES & QUESTIONS

READING LOGS

Title

Author

Genre

Format: ○ Paper ○ E-book ○ Audio

Where/When Read ______

FIRST THOUGHTS

FINAL IMPRESSIONS

RATINGS

Characters	Plot	Writing	Overall
☆☆☆☆☆	☆☆☆☆☆	☆☆☆☆☆	☆☆☆☆☆

Recommend: ○ Yes ○ No Why: ______

NOTES & QUESTIONS

NOTES & QUESTIONS

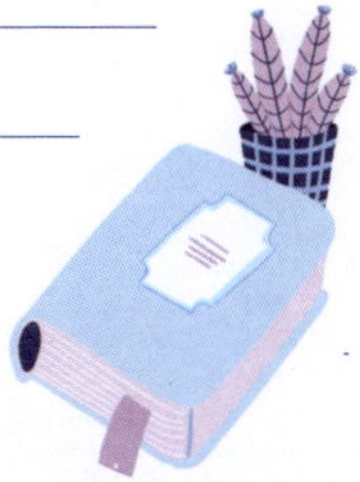

READING LOG INDEX

Page#	Title	Author	Date Read	Overall Rating
				☆☆☆☆☆
				☆☆☆☆☆
				☆☆☆☆☆
				☆☆☆☆☆
				☆☆☆☆☆
				☆☆☆☆☆
				☆☆☆☆☆
				☆☆☆☆☆
				☆☆☆☆☆
				☆☆☆☆☆
				☆☆☆☆☆
				☆☆☆☆☆
				☆☆☆☆☆
				☆☆☆☆☆

Page#	Title	Author	Date Read	Overall Rating
				☆☆☆☆☆
				☆☆☆☆☆
				☆☆☆☆☆
				☆☆☆☆☆
				☆☆☆☆☆
				☆☆☆☆☆
				☆☆☆☆☆
				☆☆☆☆☆
				☆☆☆☆☆
				☆☆☆☆☆
				☆☆☆☆☆
				☆☆☆☆☆
				☆☆☆☆☆
				☆☆☆☆☆

READING LOG INDEX

Page#	Title	Author	Date Read	Overall Rating
				☆☆☆☆☆
				☆☆☆☆☆
				☆☆☆☆☆
				☆☆☆☆☆
				☆☆☆☆☆
				☆☆☆☆☆
				☆☆☆☆☆
				☆☆☆☆☆
				☆☆☆☆☆
				☆☆☆☆☆
				☆☆☆☆☆
				☆☆☆☆☆
				☆☆☆☆☆
				☆☆☆☆☆

Page#	Title	Author	Date Read	Overall Rating
				☆☆☆☆☆
				☆☆☆☆☆
				☆☆☆☆☆
				☆☆☆☆☆
				☆☆☆☆☆
				☆☆☆☆☆
				☆☆☆☆☆
				☆☆☆☆☆
				☆☆☆☆☆

START CLUBBING!

Whether you're reading sci-fi thrillers with another friend, academic papers with a study group, or romance novels alone, *My Book Club Journal* helps you remember your reads and focus your thoughts. Recalling the good (and not-so-good) parts of books you've read with others is a great way to keep the book fresh in your mind and keep you engaged in reading. If you're looking to start your own club, here are a few things to consider.

Who

How many people will be joining your club? One other person? A large group? Who you invite will determine when, where, how often you can meet, and, to a certain extent, what you will be reading.

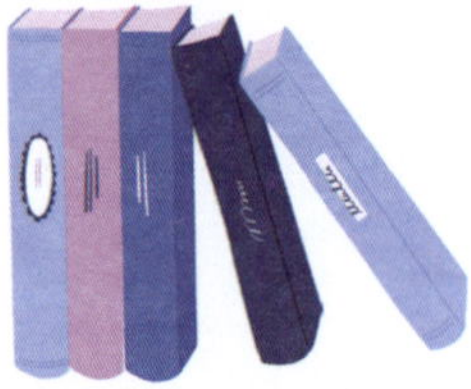

Tips for Finding Your Club

- To start your own club, make a short list of people—friends, family, colleagues—who may be interested in joining. Invite two or three friends, and if you'd like a larger club, ask them to invite a member of their own.

- New to the area, or don't know many people? Check out community boards, local online forums, and local social media spaces to find those interested in participating in a book club.

- Check your local library, community center, or local bookstore—online or in person—to see if there are any postings for a book club in your area. If you're looking to start your own club, create flyers with the relevant information and ask if you can promote your club in commmunity spaces. When in doubt, ask your local librarian or community center staff member for assistance!

- If you're ready to be part of a club but not ready to create one, online book clubs are a great way to start getting involved. Many celebrities such as Oprah Winfrey run clubs through their apps, and platforms such as Goodreads run clubs that members can participate in at their leisure.

Why

Why, ultimately, are members choosing to meet? While some prefer to focus on the book at hand, others find the socialization and snacks the core of their club. That's okay! Before you begin diving into any required reading, meet with potential members and ask them about their expectations—not only how much reading they would like to do but also how much time should be spent talking about the selection per meeting.

What

What genre(s) will you be reading? Fiction or nonfiction? Casual or academic? Though these answers may evolve over time, having a sense of what you'd like to read will influence who—and how many people—you invite.

Deciding What to Read

- Come up with a list of genres and/or topics you're interested in. Present your list to your fellow readers and discuss what you'd like to explore first. Remember to keep an open mind!

- A good book club gives everyone the opportunity to read what they'd like. After each book, rotate the person who selects the next read. For larger groups, invite members to pick three titles they're interested in and select your next read through ranked-choice voting or random selection.

When

How often would you like to meet? The more people participating, the more schedules will need coordinating. Start with monthly meetings and assess frequency as needed. Shorter books might be discussed over the course of one long meeting. Longer books may benefit from having multiple brief check-ins to talk about developments and encourage readers to stay committed. Some books such as mysteries may benefit from multiple meetings to discuss plot twists and predictions.

Where

Clubbing online? Think about how you'll set up your digital space. Which website or platform will you use? Will you be communicating through email, text, video, phone, or a combination? Depending on the platform, creating an ongoing discussion will be essential in keeping members engaged. Start new threads, create polls or challenges, and take the time to thoughtfully reply to others' comments. If chatting over video, be sure to test your network connection beforehand and give your computer time to update your software, if necessary.

Clubbing in person? Keep in mind the number of members in your group and choose a location that best suits your needs.

- Libraries, community centers, and independent bookstores may have spaces to accommodate your group but often require you to reserve a room in advance. Be sure to check with employees on space availability and how far out reservations need to be made.

- Cafes and restaurants are great meeting spots for larger, more social book clubs, though you and others may need to reserve a spot in advance and will be required to purchase food or drinks. The noise level of the restaurant may affect readers' concentration and limit discussion.

- Outdoor spaces such as parks are an excellent way to make the most of any warm, sunny weather and are great for large and small groups alike. Be sure to keep an eye on the weather report the week of the meeting and have a backup location in case conditions worsen. A few days prior, ask members if they can provide blankets or pillows for seating, as well as snacks and beverages to stay nourished and hydrated. Don't forget the sunscreen!

- If clubbing at a private residence, you may want to take turns hosting in-person meetings. Always give your members ample time to prepare by setting up a rotating schedule or choosing a host at least a week or two in advance. If you are hosting your club, be sure to provide refreshments, seating, and materials such as notebooks and pens for members who may need them. If you're attending a meeting at another residence, ask the host if they would like members to bring anything such as food or drinks.

How

Starting or joining a book club is one thing but participating is another. Be prepared to ask questions, provide evidence for your opinions, and steer conversation away from unproductive or inflammatory discussion. Check out the tips on the following pages for keeping discussions engaging and polite.

Ask questions. They aren't just a way to explore different opinions. Asking questions to shyer members, or those overshadowed by more domineering members, can help ensure that everyone has the opportunity to speak.

Listen and interpret. Allow the person talking to speak their full thought without interruption. Build on what others say and acknowledge their observations and opinions. Ask questions in a calm, rational manner. If you do not understand, rephrase their comment, framing it with the words "it seems," to give them the opportunity to clarify your interpretation: "It seems to me that what so-and-so is trying to say is..."

Take notes. While reading, mark passages, pages, quotes, and anything that strikes you—whether it be funny, insightful, or incomprehensible. Think about why this caught your attention and bring up the reason for marking it at meetings. During discussion, take notes on what was said—and who said what. Taking notes not only keeps everyone engaged but also refreshes everyone's memory on previous discussions.

Keep a calm, open mind. Inevitably, members may disagree on the material or on things said during the book club. Everyone reads differently, but all members deserve to be treated with respect. The key to navigating heated discussions is to keep things focused, polite, and calm.

Be polite if you disagree. Never insult your members with dismissive comments or personal attacks. If you disagree with someone, avoid negative subjective words like, "wrong," and "bad," and especially avoid demoralizing terms like, "stupid". A simple, "I'm not sure I agree with that," followed by your evidence-backed opinion, is a polite way to disagree while being respectful.

If the discussion becomes unproductive, don't linger. Instead, acknowledge that you cannot come to a consensus, offer to talk further after the meeting, and pivot to a new topic to keep the conversation moving.

RECOMMENDED READING

Not sure where to start? Check out the following lists to provide inspiration for titles, authors, genres, or subjects that may interest you.

Prize-Winning Fiction

The Overstory by Richard Powers (2018)
The Underground Railroad by Colson Whitehead (2016)
The Sympathizer by Viet Thanh Nguyen (2015)
The Road by Cormac McCarthy (2006)
Beloved by Toni Morrison (1987)
The Color Purple by Alice Walker (1982)
To Kill a Mockingbird by Harper Lee (1960)
The Old Man and the Sea by Ernest Hemingway (1952)
The Grapes of Wrath by John Steinbeck (1939)
The Age of Innocence by Edith Wharton (1920)

Prize-Winning Nonfiction

Evicted: Poverty and Profit in the American City by Matthew Desmond (2016)
Between the World and Me by Ta-Nehisi Coates (2015)
Behind the Beautiful Forevers by Katherine Boo (2012)
The Warmth of Other Suns by Isabel Wilkerson (2010)
The Dead Hand: The Untold Story of the Cold War Arms Race and Its Dangerous Legacy by David E. Hoffman (2009)
Slavery by Another Name: The Re-Enslavement of Black Americans from the Civil War to World War II by Douglas A. Blackmon (2008)
The Looming Tower by Lawrence Wright (2006)

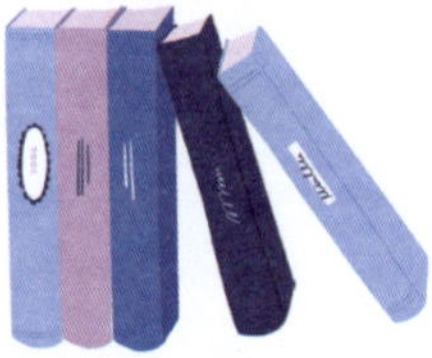

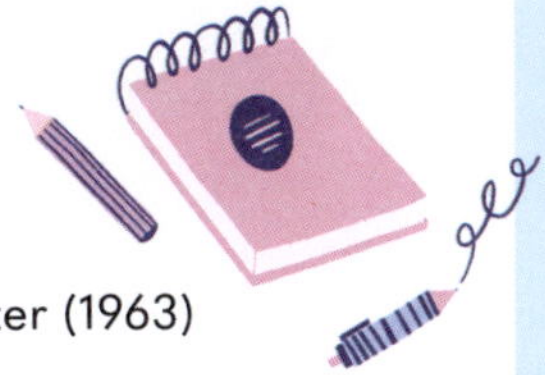

The Year of Magical Thinking by Joan Didion (2005)
The Dragons of Eden by Carl Sagan (1977)
Anti-intellectualism in American Life by Richard Hofstadter (1963)

21st Century Bestsellers

Crying in H Mart by Michelle Zauner (2021)
Gone Girl by Gillian Flynn (2012)
Thinking, Fast and Slow by Daniel Kahneman (2011)
The Immortal Life of Henrietta Lacks by Rebecca Skloot (2010)
The Art of Racing in the Rain by Garth Stein (2008)
The God Delusion by Richard Dawkins (2006)
The Girl with the Dragon Tattoo by Stieg Larsson (2005)
Wolf Totem by Jiang Rong (2004)
The Kite Runner by Khaled Hosseini (2003)
Life of Pi by Yann Martel (2001)

The Classics

The Master and Margarita by Mikhail Bulgakov (1967)
In Cold Blood by Truman Capote (1966)
One Flew Over the Cuckoo's Nest by Ken Kesey (1962)
Things Fall Apart by Chinua Achebe (1958)
The Chrysalids by John Wyndham (1955)
Nineteen Eighty-Four by George Orwell (1949)
Their Eyes Were Watching God by Zora Neale Hurston (1937)
Brave New World by Aldous Huxley (1932)
To the Lighthouse by Virginia Woolf (1927)
The Great Gatsby by F. Scott Fitzgerald (1925)

RECOMMENDED READING

The Classics (continued)

The Call of the Wild by Jack London (1903)
Crime and Punishment by Fyodor Dostoevsky (1866)
Jane Eyre by Charlotte Brontë (1847)
Frankenstein by Mary Shelley (1818)
Pride and Prejudice by Jane Austen (1813)
The Art of War by Sun Tzu

Children's Books Every Adult Should Read

The Hate U Give by Angie Thomas (2017)
The Fault in Our Stars by John Green (2012)
The Boy in the Striped Pajamas by John Boyne (2006)
Coraline by Neil Gaiman (2002)
Haroun and the Sea of Stories by Salman Rushdie (1990)
Roll of Thunder, Hear My Cry by Mildred D. Taylor (1976)
The Lion, the Witch and the Wardrobe by C. S. Lewis (1950)
The Little Prince by Antoine de Saint-Exupéry (1943)
Anne of Green Gables by Lucy Maud Montgomery (1908)
Peter Pan by J. M. Barrie (1911)
Alice's Adventures in Wonderland by Lewis Carroll (1865)

Ambitious Reads

Cloud Atlas by David Mitchell (2004)

Infinite Jest by David Foster Wallace (1996)

Gravity's Rainbow by Thomas Pynchon (1973)

One Hundred Years of Solitude by Gabriel García Márquez (1967)

Atlas Shrugged by Ayn Rand (1957)

Ulysses by James Joyce (1922)

The Sound and the Fury by William Faulkner (1929)

Les Misérables by Victor Hugo (1862)

Moby-Dick by Herman Melville (1851)

The Canterbury Tales by Geoffrey Chaucer (1392)

My BOOK CLUB Journal

weldonowen
www.weldonowen.com

Illustrations by Jessica Smith
Art Direction and Design by Ashley Quackenbush
Text by Jourdan Plautz

ISBN: 978-1-68188-964-1

MANUFACTURED IN CHINA
10 9 8